Keeping Count

Written by Claire Owen

India

My name is Nadira. My family comes from Pakistan, but now we live in India. Just about every day, we use numerals. Why are numerals important? Where did our number system come from?

Contents

Wherever you see me, you'll find activities to try and questions to answer.

The Indus Valley

The name *India* comes from the *Indus* River,
a large river in what was once northwest India.
About 4,000 years ago, the Indus Valley had two
great cities named Mohenjo-Daro and Harappa,
as well as many villages and towns. The people
farmed animals and grew crops of wheat, barley,
peas, sesame, and cotton. They used special ovens
to bake bricks, and they had tools made of bronze.

Ancient city of Mohenjo-Daro

Harappa

Mohenjo-Daro

Indus River

INDUS VALLEY

INDIA

The people of the Indus Valley had a system of weights and measures. What kinds of things do you think they measured?

Did You Know?

In the Indus Valley, clay tags were used to seal bundles of goods. While the clay was wet, a merchant would press his seal into it, leaving an imprint.

Archaeologists have found many ancient seals that show picture writing. So far, no one has been able to figure out what this writing means, but some of the symbols are thought to show numbers.

Left: Merchant's seal
Right: Clay tag with imprint of seal

archaeologist a scientist who
studies things left
by ancient peoples

Indian Numerals

The number symbols discovered by archaeologists in the Indus Valley were like tally marks. Indian numerals changed over time. About 2,000 years later, people were using Brahmi numerals. After another 600 years, a place-value number system that used Hindu numerals had been developed.

Brahmi Numerals

1	2	3	4	5	6	7	8	9
—	=	≡	Ɏ	ſ	ϐ	ʔ	५	ʔ

In addition to these numerals, there were special symbols for "tens" (10, 20, … 90) and for the numbers 100 and 1,000.

Hindu Numerals

1	2	3	4	5	6	7	8	9	0
٦	?	३	४	५	८	ʔ	٢	ᴓ	ο

These symbols, or digits, could be used to write any numeral. For example, 293 would be ?ᴓ३.
Today, we write numerals in a similar way, using the digits 0 to 9.

numeral a symbol that represents a number

A

B

C

D

E

On the seals above, which symbols do you think show numbers? What do you think the other symbols might mean?

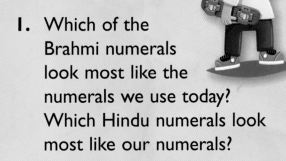

1. Which of the Brahmi numerals look most like the numerals we use today? Which Hindu numerals look most like our numerals?

2. Write these Hindu numbers in figures and then in words.

   a. ३७   b. ५२

   c. ८२२   d. ७०४

   e. २३८५ f. ४०६२

3. Design your own seal. (You could draw it or make it from clay.) Make sure that it shows a number.

Arabic Numerals

In the year 767, some Indian astronomers visited the Middle East. There, they showed Arabian astronomers the Hindu number system. The Arabs began to use this system, which made it easier to work with large numbers. Over the years, the numerals continued to change a little.

astronomer   a person who studies stars, planets, comets, and other objects in the universe

Arabic Numerals

1	2	3	4	5	6	7	8	9	0
١	٢	٣	٤	٥	٦	٧	٨	٩	٠

Hindu-Arabic Numerals

Today, most people in the world use Hindu-Arabic numerals.

1	2	3	4	5	6	7	8	9	0
1	2	3	4	5	6	7	8	9	0

Using Hindu numerals, mathematicians invented written methods that helped them work more quickly. This illustration from the year 1508 shows a competition between two mathematicians. One man is using numerals, and the other man is using a counting board (abacus).

mathematician   a person who studies numbers and other areas of mathematics

Place Value

In a place-value number system, the value of a digit depends on its place. For example, the 6 in 67 means six tens, or 60. The 6 in 3,687 means six hundreds, or 600. In number systems that do not use place value, it can take a lot of space to write large numbers. For example, the Roman numeral for 4,687 is MMMMDCLXXXVII!

Roman numerals a number system that uses letters to represent numbers (I = one, V = five, X = ten, L = fifty, C = one hundred, D = five hundred, M = one thousand)

Playing "Three Digits"

To play "Three Digits," two players will need 10 digit cards, like these:

1. Turn the cards face-down and mix them together.

2. Each player draws boxes for a three-digit number.

3. Players take turns picking a card and writing the digit in one of the boxes. (The aim of the game is to make the greatest possible number.)

Hmm ... 3 is a small number, so I don't want to write it in the hundreds column ....

4. In between turns, the cards are mixed again.

5. After three rounds, the player with the greater number scores one point.

I win!

840   773

Play the game again. The first player with five points wins.

Number Systems

Different number systems developed in different parts of the world. Some of the systems used place value, but not all of them were decimal systems. Each system had a different way of writing or showing numbers.

The Maya of Central America had special symbols for the numbers 0 to 19.

The Inca people of Peru tied knots on strings called *quipu* to show the number of hundreds, tens, ones, and so on.

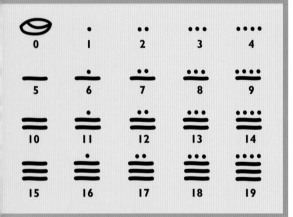

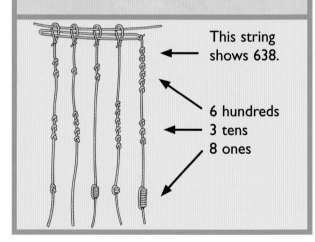

This string shows 638.

6 hundreds
3 tens
8 ones

decimal system a number system based on 10

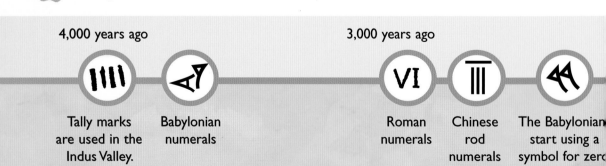

4,000 years ago

3,000 years ago

Tally marks are used in the Indus Valley.

Babylonian numerals

Roman numerals

Chinese rod numerals

The Babylonian start using a symbol for zero

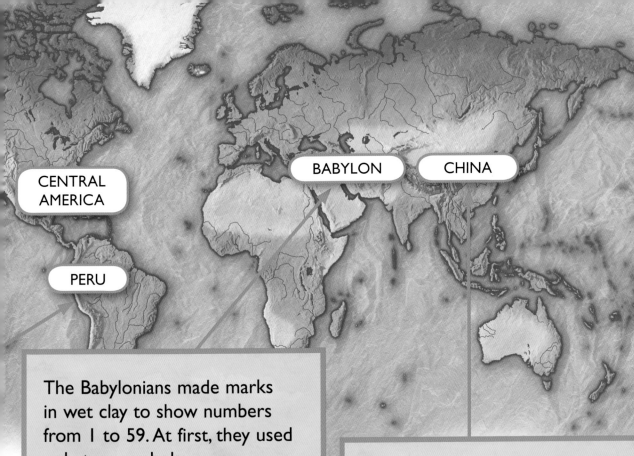

CENTRAL
AMERICA

BABYLON   CHINA

PERU

The Babylonians made marks
in wet clay to show numbers
from 1 to 59. At first, they used
only two symbols:

𒑊 = 1   𒌋 = 10

Here is the number 25:

The Chinese used sticks
or rods to show numbers.

| | || | ||| | |||| | ||||| | ⊤ | ⊤⊤ | ⊤⊤⊤ | ⊤⊤⊤⊤ |
| 1 | 2 | 3 | 4 | 5 | 6 | 7 | 8 | 9 |

00 years ago   1,000 years ago   Today

        ？ๆ】   2ヨ၅

Brahmi   Maya   Hindu   The Arabs   The Inca tie   We use
numerals   numerals   numerals   learn about   knots on   Hindu-Arabic
                                    Hindu   quipu to show   numbers.
                                    numerals.   numbers.

13

Everyday Numbers

Today, we use numbers more than ever before. Numerals are all around us—at home, at school, at work, at the store, and at the mall. Numerals show measurements, times, and prices. They can also be used as codes or labels. Without numerals, the world would be a very different place!

Ais 6

1,000 items on sale!

$0.75

$0.60

Oranges 2lbs. for $2.50

2lbs

Tomatoes 2lbs. for $3.00

Today's Specials

Bananas 1 lb. for $0.70

$1.25

$2.20

$2.20

$2.20

$2.20

$2.20

$2.20

$5.

Sample Answers

Page 7   **2.**   a.   39; thirty-nine

b.   52; fifty-two

c.   681; six hundred and eighty-one

d.   104; one hundred and four

e.   2,345; two thousand three hundred and forty-five

f.   4,088; four thousand and eighty-eight

Find out more about Chinese or Maya numerals, or find out about the number system used by the ancient Egyptians.

Index